Index

Trading System 3

    The evolution of Trading Systems from the 1990s to today 12

    Money Management 19

    The main types of Trading System 31

Chapter 2 - The pros and cons of the Trading System..52

    2.1 – Advantages......................................57

    2.2 – Disadvantages 65

Chapter 3 - How to build a successful Trading System..73

    3.1 – Market analysis and basic principles 79

    3.2 – Logical schemes and testing............90

    3.3 – Possible mistakes to avoid 102

Conclusions 107

Trading System

The world of trading is aimed at buying and selling financial instruments on the stock exchange and in stock markets, speculating on price changes. The technological evolution that has taken place in recent decades has sanctioned the transition from manual trading to online trading, both discretionary and based on the use of automated tools. Online trading can be a valuable tool to generate profits, but at the same time it can be a pitfall for inexperienced traders who are driven by the illusion that such profits can be obtained quickly and without any effort. To overcome this possibility, it is important to use analysis tools and efficient software that are able to test the validity of the strategies adopted. The objective is to obtain gains from the opening and closing of up or down transactions, limiting the risk of incurring huge losses that would inevitably squander one's capital.

Trading is an activity that should not be underestimated, as it can be counted among the most complex jobs in the financial world. The implications it brings go beyond the economic sphere, embracing above all the psychological and emotional.

For this reason, automated trading systems, the so-called Trading Systems, have been designed in such a way as to eliminate the typical anxiogenic component of man, to allow for greater clarity and validity of operations. Eliminating discretion is therefore the first step to implement a valid trading strategy.

However, even this new type of trading is not infallible, therefore it is essential to deepen the skills of statistics, mathematics and finance. Furthermore, if you opt for a free Trading System platform, you will be guaranteed lower efficiency compared to paid platforms, which however have high costs. However, the proper assumption of trading is the investment, which is the basis of the whole process: without an initial investment, it will not be possible to start any valid trading strategy. If you do not want to opt for an already packaged system, it is possible to build a Trading System from scratch, setting the most suitable parameters and indicators for the strategy you intend to implement. In this case, you will also need to learn the basics of computer programming and languages, to implement the codes and algorithms necessary for the system, or alternatively you can turn to expert programmers, with the various risks involved.

Pursuing a strategy valid in the world of automated trading, can prove profitable in the long run, as only with perseverance and perseverance will it be possible to become professional traders able to exploit all the financial market trends in their favor, albeit with negative phases , which will however in most cases be more than offset by positive ones.

Chapter 1 - What is a Trading System

The financial markets are characterized by a series of risks that potential investors must necessarily know and evaluate, through the study of financial strategies and techniques and the analysis of temporal and personal factors, which can affect the risk appetite. It is also necessary to identify the assets to be included in the financial portfolio, such as for example shares, bonds and other derivative securities. The winning strategy of every investor, also called a trader, is based on choosing the best time to sell or buy securities, based on accurate oscillators, indicators and analyzes.

However, observing all the financial combinations at the same time and being able to choose the optimal time to carry out your investment is complex, as the market often presents pitfalls. Precisely for this reason, automated trading systems have recently emerged.

The Trading System is an automatic trading system, which allows the sales and purchase signals to be processed in a totally objective manner in a short time, through the combination of technical and statistical indicators, to contain the risk and maximize profitability.

It is possible to carry out the Trading System through specific software, able to translate and process in real time the rules that the trader decides to adopt to move in the financial markets. Therefore it is the trader who decides which events will trigger the activation of the automatic trading system. What differentiates the Trading System from traditional trading is the total absence of the emotional element: in fact, the trader inevitably suffers emotional consequences after each investment, which can lead him, for example, to take excessive risk due to the desire for redemption to following a previous negative trade.

However, the software does not totally eliminate the risk, but rather ponders it, both in the short and medium and long term.

The evolution of Trading Systems from the 1990s to today

In the 1990s, before the advent of online trading, making financial transactions was rather complex, as it was necessary to use an intermediary, called a broker, or your own bank, to place sales or purchase orders.

The cumbersome nature of the system and the financial market did not allow traders to easily incorporate information, such as those relating to prices, in a short time. This slowness also affected the time needed to place orders, in fact sometimes they even spent a few days, with the risk that prices would change in the meantime. This was partly due to the fact that orders could only be executed by telephone or physically at the bank's securities counters. Traders also had to incur costs and commissions much higher than those of today's online trading. To all this was added the impossibility of carrying out economic analyzes of the markets, making each investment highly risky.

The trading market has undergone a profound change since the end of the 1990s, thanks to the spread of computers and the Internet. In recent years we have witnessed the growth of online trading systems, through platforms specially created by banks and SIMs, to which investors could freely access from home, operating in the markets quickly and easily.

In order to facilitate investments and streamline technical times, many brokers have established affiliations with banks, so as to connect the various accounts held by the trader. These simplifications, in addition to the considerable reduction in the costs related to the commissions due for each individual trading transaction, have led to a significant increase in the number of traders on the market. Some of them managed to make investments and financial operations a real job, others instead, acting without a real trading strategy and lacking sufficient knowledge of the market, have progressively depleted their capital.

What distinguishes the financial market, particularly in the years from 2000 to 2007, is the possibility of opening positions on transactions characterized by a very short duration, sometimes even a few minutes. The traders who implemented a strategy of this kind, based on so-called scalping, aimed to monetize fairly modest amounts of money, as quickly as possible. In reality, these strategies have spread the illusion, both among experienced traders and beginners, of creating net profit within a few hours, with a rather contained initial investment and with a weighted and acceptable risk, but realizing actual gains only for the brokers. In fact, with the opening of the financial market to the world of the web the inexperienced traders have increased who, with a limited budget, have tried to make a fortune, ending up losing the capital they had decided to invest: the percentage of these subjects is around to 90% of all traders; however, over the years, even the few winning traders have gradually decreased.

Only in 2008 were machines introduced into the financial market, with the aim of reducing risks and errors and in order to optimize the search for information, even if the first systems had been implemented in the United States already at the end of the 1990s trading coded through the use of software. The transition to the Trading System was in some ways revolutionary, thanks to the possibility of scanning an almost unlimited number of transactions quickly.

Thanks to the implementation of automated trading software, generally programmed in C ++ or JavaScript language, it is possible to analyze every aspect of the financial market and exploit every investment potential. The use of these software has allowed even the less experienced subjects to take the way of online trading to try to make a profit, greatly reducing the risks.

Money Management

Money Management can be considered as the plan for the allocation, management and protection of one's capital for various investments.

The allocation of capital is nothing but the set of decisions relating to the amount of resources to be allocated to a specific type of financial instrument. The choice is influenced by certain factors, such as risk appetite and the amount of initial capital. But not only. It is very important that the trader evaluates from the beginning the amount of time he wants to invest and the state of the financial markets. All this can be enclosed in the concept of position sizing, which allows you to monitor investments at a precise moment, in order to control risk and manage savings. The position sizing suggests for this reason not to allocate a percentage higher than 5% compared to its portfolio, to a single investment.

The Trading Systems offer valid strategies for efficient capital management and to guarantee profits over time. Through the Trading Systems and through market or sector differentiation, it is possible to implement different strategies also on the same securities, acting on the variables of return and risk, as it is not a gambling, but an investment. The combined use of several Trading Systems can therefore implement the principle of differentiation, thus allowing to optimally manage the allocated capital, maximizing the ratio between yield and risk. Once you have implemented your ideal system, by using one or more Trading Systems according to the different prospects of future income, the simple management of capital becomes real risk management. This concept is fundamental to define the analysis of possible risks and to be aware of the position occupied in the financial market.

The last fundamental phase of Money Management is instead that of capital protection. This is a delicate moment, as the trader must be able to manage the investments made: this means knowing the exact moment in which to close a given transaction, be it at a loss or a profit. Also during this phase traders can rely on Trading Systems, which are able to optimize every single investment strategy.

The decision to close a position is fundamental not only for what concerns the optimization of profit, but also to avoid seeing the entire investment allocated for that particular transaction vain. The world of trading contemplates the possibility of making bad investments, as they are an integral part of the financial market: however, the trader must be good at understanding in advance when the time is right to minimize the loss. Even if this decision is delegated to a Trading System, the trader must still have sufficient knowledge of the market and of the closing mechanism of the transaction and, consequently, of the capital protection strategy.

In fact implementing a strategy containing certain exit conditions from the outset is in some ways more useful than a strategy with excellent entry conditions.

It therefore becomes essential to exploit all the signals of modern automated trading systems, in order to optimize Money Management and the strategy adopted. Signals can be grouped into five specific categories:

- Stop Loss. This is a signal capable of limiting the losses related to each operation performed. However it will be up to the trader to define how the Trading System should close the position, and this can happen when a certain fixed percentage is calculated based on the total invested capital, or in the event that the loss reaches a certain value that exceeds the percentage calculated on the basis of the volatility of the financial security, or even exceeding a fixed amount, if the investment concerns derivative financial instruments.

- Breakeven Stop. Through this signal a trader can close a balanced position once he has reached the profit previously set in the system. This reduces the risk that can arise from a sudden market reversal, but at the same time, closing the position could lead to it exiting before a favorable trend occurs.

- Trailing Stop. This signal represents the evolution of the two previous ones: the Trading System may decide to re-enter the transaction in such a way as to further exploit the positive trend of the closed position in advance. The trader will therefore have to set a certain entry level, necessarily at a higher point than the Breakeven Stop, and a new exit level, lower than the profit earned in the previous position.

- Take Profit. It is a signal similar to the previous one, the only difference lies in the fact that Take Profit contains a maximum profit level which, once reached, determines the closing of the operation. This signal is particularly useful if the trader decides to operate within a fairly narrow market, while proving to be limiting if it is used in markets characterized by large trends.

- Shock Protection. The financial market is one of the markets most susceptible to external events, also due to the wide volatility of its component instruments. To prevent a sudden event from generating a trend change that could affect the profit achieved up to that point, the Shock Protection automates the closing of the position when it exceeds a value range previously established by the trader.

In Money Management it is fundamental to define the expected loss and profit forecasts, ie to quantify how much the trader expects to win or lose, which is why it is essential to use two formulas, Kelly's formula and Larry Williams formula . The first arose in the field of gambling, to maximize the profit of bets in the long run, and only later was it associated with the financial market. It takes into consideration the probabilities of obtaining a profit from each share and the average value of each positively or negatively closed action. The second one instead considers the capital and the percentage of risk, which are compared to the so-called drawdown, ie the amount of money that you are willing to lose.

The study of a valid Money Management lays the foundation for increasing the profitability of trading investments. Both the simplification of the analysis and the study of a valid and effective strategy in the financial market, and the use of signals that allow the protection of the accumulated or previously invested capital, have ensured that many traders obtain safer profits. This is mainly due to the strategic diversification that prevails in the method and in the effectiveness compared to the pure and simple investment, based on intuition and on the analytical study of the market.

The main types of Trading System

The Trading Systems can be divided into different categories, depending on the strategies that the trader intends to adopt in the financial market at a precise moment. Each category has favorable and unfavorable elements, therefore the trader must be able to choose the most suitable type for managing his own Money Management.

Each of the types of Trading System is valid like all the others, as there is no better strategy than another, but the effectiveness of each of them is closely related to market conditions at the time the trader makes the 'investment.

The use of the Trading System has a dual aspect, on the one hand it represents a tool capable of supporting decisions, on the other it performs the function of an operational tool with respect to the reports generated.

The main Trading System models can be identified in Trend Following systems, in systems with opposite trends or inversion and in systems characterized by volatility.

1.3.1 – Trend Following

The Trend Following model is the type most used by traders in the financial market. Thanks to these models it is in fact possible to identify trends, having been developed for this purpose. If the system is able to capture a defined trend, the percentage of positive transactions is very high and generates the maximum benefit from the primary trend. The signals, however, are not always timely with respect to the minimums and the maximums of the period, and this aspect can bring difficulties.

The pursuit of trends, however, can generate large losses in the so-called lateral market phases, especially in the rather long-lasting ones, since the obstinacy of these systems to follow the trend at any cost can generate higher costs than the benefits. It may be useful to include wide stop-loss levels in order to limit the instability of the trend, but this is not always sufficient, especially if one operates in non-directional markets characterized by a high level of volatility.

To implement a valid Trend Following strategy it is necessary to identify a strong trend on the market, through the use of some indicators, among all the moving average, which highlights the average price of a financial instrument in a given time interval, identifying the upward phases , those of decline and those of trading range.

A Trend Following oscillator based on the moving average is the Triple Index or Trix, which detects the percentage change of a triple exponential moving average estimated on the closing price. The Trix varies around the trigger line, ie at zero, picking up purchase signals above it and opening signals downwards below. But not only. If the market is in an overbought or oversold phase, the oscillator will be able to highlight both depreciation and appreciation.

Depending on the market entry signals, it is possible to distinguish two different trend followers, namely the Breakout traders and the Swing traders.

The Breakout traders are activated when a so-called uptrend occurs, ie when the price exceeds a certain level, be it minimum or maximum, closing beyond a certain resistance. At this time, entry into the market takes place automatically. In the same way, with the downward trend of the trend, the stop loss tends to assume lower and lower recent values until it takes on the value of stop profit. Once the price exceeds this level, the Breakout traders close the position. Alternatively, the trader can decide to use the Bollinger bands, which not only analyze the volatility of the financial market at the time of the investment, but also study the standard deviations that act as bands to establish the opportune moment to exit the market. This trend follower has very broad time horizons, being able to vary from the very long to the very short term.

Based on the duration of the trend, it is possible to distinguish three types of Breakout traders: Position traders, Momentum traders and Scalpers.

Position traders operate over the long term, through an accurate technical analysis of weekly or monthly charts, without taking into consideration intraday fluctuations.

The Momentum traders exploit the price changes of the trend only for a few days and in phases that tend to be significant or of high volatility.

The traders who instead operate in the very short term are called Scalpers, and can get to carry out hundreds of operations with a duration equal to or less than a minute over a single day, obtaining small profits from time to time.

What activates the second trend follower, namely the swing traders, is not the overcoming of a resistance or the stop profit, but the slowing of the trend of a trend, defined in technical jargon swing. In fact, the tendential deceleration of the market can provide indications on possible restarts and, if the necessary conditions are met, the trend follower reignites the position before the trend resumes its trend.

1.3.2 – The reversal

Pursuing the trend is certainly the strategy most used by traders who invest in the financial market using Trading Systems, but not the only one for this. Strategies based on inversion, for example, represent a very valid alternative, especially for the high probability of success. This strategy is mainly adopted by traders who decide to opt for mechanical trading. What makes these strategies less appealing is the lower average gain linked to each individual trading operation, even if the opposite trend systems guarantee lower risks, especially during the lateral phases of the trend. Of course also the inversion systems base their activation on some oscillators, but they also rely on some patterns that, compared to the logics that guide the Trend Following strategies, turn out to be much more concrete. Ultimately, trend reversal systems attempt to take advantage of the so-called rebound phase. So if a trend follows a constantly rising logic, the strategy requires investing by opening downward positions, and vice versa. The Trading System will therefore act in advance with respect to the possible variation of the trend, unlike the Trend Following which instead tends to follow the direction taken by the trend in a stubborn manner.

There are multiple systems based on a trend reversal strategy. One of the main methods bases its analysis on the comparison of the divergences between real price and that expected from the main stochastic oscillators. Specifically, a reversal signal can be generated when prices reach a new low, the trend continues to fall into oversold and the oscillator rises, thus creating a trend reversal. The same applies to the opposite case.

An additional Reverse Trading System method is known as the Ultimate Oscillator, and was designed and implemented by Larry Williams. This system differs from any other oscillator in that it is able to compare and analyze the prices of a specific financial instrument in three different time intervals. In this way the oscillator will be able to identify with greater certainty the moments in which the trend reversals will occur.

Of course, the patterns are very important, which allow the Trading Systems to hypothesize what the behavior of prices will be in the successive time intervals in the financial market. What traders prefer are patterns that have a particular significance from a statistical point of view, depending on the frequency with which they appear on the market. Furthermore, the patterns must be rigorously codable by means of the computer programming languages used by the Trading Systems: therefore their regulation must not be ambiguous or random, but certain and determined. In order to satisfy both requirements, the patterns must have less than three or four bars. Once developed they will surely be the most immediate manifestation of the purchase and sale relationships on the financial market and, consequently, the possibilities of identifying the price level in the successive time intervals will considerably increase.

1.3.3 – Volatility

Another type of trading system is based on the concept of volatility, which is important for achieving greater success both in short-term investments and in medium and long-term trading. Volatility is nothing more than the standard deviation and as such manifests the variation that a given price undergoes on the financial market in a precise time interval. This parameter is fundamental not only for the trader who wants to invest his capital but for the Trading Systems themselves which thanks to it are able to analyze the variation in the returns of the category of financial products observed on the market. Following this logic, volatility represents the risk inherent in a trading transaction, being the same two parameters that are proportional to each other.

Interpreting volatility through the standard deviation indicator is useful for traders to evaluate the best time to enter the market: in fact, if it presents too low values and therefore the market is in a flat phase, a surge may soon occur. Business; vice versa, if it has high values, it is likely that a slowdown in activity will occur shortly.

It is important to distinguish the "good" volatility from the "bad" volatility, to avoid being misled by the market: the former in fact generates gains when it is intercepted correctly, while the latter activates the stop loss following a entry in the long run before the market changes trend and resumes the upward trend. For this reason the Trading Systems must be able to filter the volatility to operate optimally.

This type of Trading System probably presents the most important oscillator, namely The Volatility Momentum. This oscillator is able to analyze the variation of the prices of the observed financial instrument and, in the same interval of time, the reaction of the whole market to the variation of the price of the single instruments. The oscillator is compared with the market volumes: from this report the moving average on which the signals of purchase and exit from the market are based is quantified. The Volatility Momentum is also recommended as a refinement of the Trend Following typology. In fact the latter presents obvious shortcomings in the investments made during the lateral phases: through the combined use of a Trend Trading System Following with the Volatility Momentum oscillator it is possible, however, to reduce the time intervals during which the trader's positions are open , so as to reduce losses.

The Volatility Breakout oscillator is less used, which aims to create a real volatility range that varies according to the financial market trend. The positive aspect of this oscillator is that it is able to create its own statistical base on which to set the signals for buying or closing the position. This statistical basis will be decisive if the market goes through rather long lateral phases, as the oscillator will keep an objective theoretical model on the future market trend, which will allow for a more accurate analysis and, consequently, a trading positive.

Chapter 2 - The pros and cons of the Trading System

Every professional trader knows that it is not possible to predict with certainty what is the trend of financial instruments on the market. It is precisely for this reason that the Trading Systems are born, as elements of objective and decisional support, which contemplate the risk factors and act accordingly. In fact they contain different trading plans and different strategies and, thanks to oscillators and signals, it is possible to act by following the best probability of achievable success. However, the responsibility for entering the conditions for opening positions and leaving the market within the Trading System still falls on traders, who must therefore have sufficient knowledge of the market trend they will operate on and the basic rules that characterize it.

The realization of the conditions cannot therefore be accidental or carried out by inexperienced subjects, as in this case one would incur the risk that the automated system opens positions in less opportune moments, or leaves the market at the time of maximum realization.

The birth of the Trading System has led many individuals to think that automated trading generates miraculous gains without too much effort and in a short time. This consideration is completely wrong, because at the base of these systems there is a complex algorithm that, through a series of logical steps, identifies the price levels at which financial products are traded. To do this, the algorithm performs a meticulous technical analysis of the oscillators and indicators.

The technological progress of the last few years has also had implications in the world of Trading System and financial market. In fact, numerous totally automatic trading platforms have been created, which directly manage securities trading and price change signals. Such platforms also allow less experienced traders to enter the world of trading, offering them the possibility of operating even from the smartphone through the appropriate applications.

The Trading Systems are therefore an evolution of the trading plans made by man. For this reason, the creation and use of automated systems has led to significant advantages for investors in the financial field. But to every pro there is a counter. The disadvantages, however small if compared to human trading, must however be contemplated and analyzed.

2.1 – Advantages

It is possible to identify a series of advantages deriving from the use of Trading System systems. The main advantage, as previously expressed, is the complete elimination of the emotional element in the context of trading operations, which characterizes man. Therefore a Trading System is based on objective criteria, thanks to which it limits human interference and allows to increase profits.

Another advantage for traders is saving time. In fact, before the advent of the Trading System, investors had to devote a large number of hours to study and market analysis, before deciding on the convenience to make an investment. These systems, on the other hand, carry out tests on the market directly and quickly, so that the trader is active only when the Trading System picks up signals of purchase or sale.

As mentioned, the decision-making process is absolutely autonomous, not being influenced by purely human factors, and implies a study of the market to be carried out following four phases, to be carried out very quickly. First of all, the Trading System must decide which is the ideal entry technique at that precise moment, be it a short or long term operation. Secondly, the Trading System must monitor the effects resulting from a possible opening of a transaction by comparing the various indicators, so as to keep under control both the success rate and the ratio between risk and return. Once the market trend and the prices of the observed financial instrument have been assessed, the automated system must make the decision in relation to the amount of capital to be used for each specific transaction, taking into consideration the entire portfolio made available by the trader. Once the position has been opened, the Trading System will still have to monitor the progress of the position, setting new stop loss points from time to time which, in the event that the percentage of risk increases excessively, can become points of exit from the market . Even if the trend proves to be positive, the Trading System will have to make the decision to exit the market before the profit is affected by a possible change of course of the trend. All this happens in a very short space of time. Any trader, albeit good, needs a much longer time to do the same job, often without considering fundamental elements or making analytical errors. The streamlining of the decision-making process thus becomes an advantage that cannot be underestimated, both in terms of time, but above all in terms of success and profit.

Furthermore, the Trading System allows you to immediately check whether the strategy you are implementing is effective or not. The strategy is analyzed in detail at any stage of the market, to understand if it is deficient in some periods, to improve the strengths, correct the weak points and solve any problems. All this can be done at no cost, simply by running simulations on a real financial market using fictitious money. Only when the trader understands that the strategy developed is the best possible, then he can open real positions with real investments.

Through the simulations it is also possible to understand what is the level of risk present on the market, obtaining, through specific analyzes carried out directly by the Trading System, the maximum loss value of the analyzed historical series and the maximum point reached by the trend. In this way the percentage of riskiness can assume real and significant data and the strategy can be further refined.

Performing different simulations before making the decision to enter the market is also useful for another reason. In fact, the Trading System must study and fix some stakes, which delimit the efficiency and convenience of the adopted strategy. If the trend analyzed breaches the limit levels set on the basis of the allocated capital and risk appetite, then the automated system immediately exits the market, interrupting the investment.

The de-responsibility of the trader can also be an advantage. The Trading Systems, in fact, are able to automatically transmit the signals of purchase and sale of the position to the brokers, without there being any type of intervention by the trader. This involves not only the possibility that the trader is not in front of the screen during all the trading phases, but also a lower level of stress for the same operator, which will be completely replaced by the system.

By eliminating the sentimental and emotional part typical of man, the Trading System allows you to make objective decisions, letting positions take full advantage of the trend when profits are obtained and interrupting the trading in the event that you begin to check for losses. The system is in fact devoid of discretion, considered perhaps the major cause of the financial errors committed by man.

2.2 – Disadvantages

However, the trading system is not made up solely of positive factors and profits. Performing trading by relying completely on algorithms and statistics can in fact result in losses that can affect the trader's capital considerably. The Trading Systems in fact must not be considered as machines generating easy money, but as executors of algorithms. The illusion therefore of obtaining high and fast profits can be considered a disadvantage for traders who will then be called upon to come to terms with reality. This false idea of the world of trading has in particular been expanded by the web which, with the aim of attracting new investors to the financial world, has boasted easy profits, thanks to almost infallible automated systems.

One of the main shortcomings of the Trading System is the difficulty in strictly complying with the strategy that the trader has set. In fact, an excellent trading follows the rule that indicates to let profits continue, without closing the position beforehand, and to cut the losses instead. This principle is respected mainly in the Trend Following systems, where even if the success rate remains relatively low, generally below 50%, the profit is still considerable, thanks to the correct cut of the losses. Furthermore, if this type of Trading System is accompanied by a filter or an oscillator capable of objectively managing capital even during the lateral market phases, the results in the medium-long term can become excellent. Many traders are looking more for the direct percentage of success, but without counting that in these cases the risk increases and the losses can be very expensive. This result is obtained when the trader, and consequently the automated system, repeatedly change his strategy, trying to refine it, but only ending up creating greater capital losses. Sometimes the trader can decide to take the situation in hand, close operations that had been opened automatically, open others that are outside the strategy implemented, but this frustrates the entire investment made and blows up the planned strategy with dedication and attention. Failure to comply with the strategic discipline is therefore an aspect that can entail numerous economic disadvantages.

However, what determines the survival of a trader in the financial market for an acceptable period of time is the ability to manage losses, both from a purely technical point of view and above all from a psychological point of view. The drawdown is in fact a difficulty that is inherent in the financial market and that even the best Trading Systems are not able to eliminate completely. The difficulty of managing capital and losses, however, can sometimes occur in the same automated systems. Even the trading systems can in fact encounter periods of total strategic destruction, of absolute darkness. During these intervals the trader will only get losses, without being able to recover the invested capital. The biggest mistake an investor can make in these cases is however to change the strategy, even if the drawdown should exceed the historical maximum.

It is possible to find some disadvantages in the use of the Trading System even in the case in which a trend changes with respect to its historical series. For this reason, many experts in the financial sector believe that it is easier and more convenient to invest in young and immature markets than in long-term and consolidated markets. The reason lies precisely in the possibility of permanently varying the time series, creating an imbalance between real data and information possessed by the automated system that causes a total blackout in the management of the portfolio.

Even in the world of trading systems, the quality of the service requires a very high cost. Many inexperienced traders try to rely, with a rather limited budget, on free trading software, available on the web. But these Trading Systems are deficient in at least two fundamental elements: firstly, the data relating to the price flows of the financial instruments analyzed are often incomplete or inaccurate and do not allow an objective market analysis to be obtained; secondly, the speed with which information is received is much lower than that possessed by automated payment systems. Quality and speed are the main components of the algorithms that should guarantee the implementation of a successful strategy. In particular, receiving inaccurate and incorrect data leads oscillators and indicators to identify key points, such as those of maxima and minima, in different positions with respect to the real ones. Therefore a trader who decides to use a poor quality Trading System has a disadvantage that is difficult to remedy.

Chapter 3 - How to build a successful Trading System

Creating a trading system from the ground up is not an easy and simple process and therefore requires considerable time. Generally, even the most experienced traders have started to appear in the trading market without a real Money Management and without having a clear idea of what would have happened once they invested their capital in a particular financial instrument.

However, few experiments are needed to understand that a strategy is needed, which can be created with simple modalities, such as adding a stop loss to test the variation of the success rate, until reaching more complex levels, perhaps crossing different moving averages. Precisely in this way, which necessarily implies the passage through various attempts, perhaps made in trading simulation channels in order not to affect the capital to be invested, the personalized money management strategy begins to take shape.

Making a Money Management is perhaps the most complicated and delicate aspect of the entire process of building the Trading Systems. The future development of its capital will depend on this strategy.

Once a strategy has been developed that is apparently able to circumvent the multiplicity of problems on the market, it is important not to change it. In fact, it is necessary to understand that there is no perfect market and investment strategy, which can totally exclude losses, but it is necessary to know how to create an algorithm capable of closing the transaction when the losses begin to occur.

Finding a balance that guarantees a relationship between yield and risk acceptable to the trader is therefore not easy, and is the result of a process that can last even many months, especially if you are at the first experience in the world of trading.

For this reason it is important, once the same market has been observed several times, to have an idea. This will serve as the basis for your Money Management and will be the fulcrum of the entire market strategy. The basic concept will be born only after understanding what really happens in the graphs and what all the elements present in them represent: therefore it is fundamental to read books dealing with trading and financial markets, in order to increase one's personal luggage.

Beginners are facing the problem on how to develop valid Trading System strategies without having programming and language notions. To facilitate this phase, some programs provide compilation assistance wizards, which allow you to set the purchase and sales parameters desired by the user. In this way it is not necessary to be an expert programmer, a fundamental requirement instead if you want to make Trading System a professional activity. In this case, traders will have to study in depth the various concepts and computer programming languages before embarking on this path. Alternatively, they can turn to specialized programmers, but run the risk that the winning idea is somehow adopted by the programmer.

Once the basic concepts of trading have been clarified, it is possible to dedicate oneself completely to the actual construction phase of a Trading System.

3.1 – Market analysis and basic principles

The first step that a trader who intends to implement a personal Trading System must implement is a market analysis. The study of the graphs, the calculation of the moving averages, the choice of the best oscillators according to the purpose to be pursued, is in fact the first step towards the realization of an automated trading system that can guarantee a gain.

The trader must therefore decide whether to opt for a Trading System that can guarantee greater chances of success, but fewer gains, such as an inversion system, or a type of system that guarantees a decidedly lower success rate, but an excellent ratio between return and risk, such as the Trend Following systems. The latter are certainly the most common and require simpler basic concepts than the other types, even if they are still complex.

The trader is also called to verify the historical series of the observed market, in order to understand which are the minimum and maximum levels of the trend.

Identifying the current trend of the trend once the moving average has been calculated is simple. The difficulty lies in understanding what the future trend of it will be. By opting for a Trend Following system this may not be a problem, as the system will stubbornly continue on the trend until there is an inversion in the trend of the series with the consequent exit from the market. Conversely, in an inversion Trading System the conditions must be set for which it is assumed that the trend will soon change trend. It is not possible to choose which system is the best a priori, as this choice depends both on the specific market in which it intends to enter and on the trader's risk appetite, and is therefore a purely personal assessment. In any case, a good Trading System must be built in a way that respects some fundamental principles: it must generate profits, it must be simple, it must be robust, it must manage risk in the most appropriate way, it must be totally automated.

The Trading System must necessarily be profitable: the average profit for each transaction and therefore its ANP, ie the Average Net Profit, must be greater than zero. This means that the gains must be constantly higher than the losses. However this is not enough. In fact, the Average Net Profit must have a positive value such as to be able to cover also the costs and the commissions related to the single transactions and to the price variations that occur between the time of the order and the actual opening of the same, the so-called slippage. Once the aforementioned costs have been subtracted, the Average Net Profit must be sufficient to offset the risk associated with trading, to guarantee a fair percentage of positive transactions even during the difficult phases of the market and to limit the loss of available capital and the consequent risk of ruin. In fact, there is an inverse relationship between the Average Net Profit and the risk of ruin: the higher the APN, the lower the risk.

Secondly, the Trading System must be based on the concept of simplicity. A trading based on a few simple rules ensures greater gains in the future, as it is more stable and effective. In fact, using complex systems can be counterproductive, as a large number of rules of behavior can lead the system to over-optimization.

A Trading System that is able to consistently generate long-term gains homogeneously regardless of market changes compared to the tests performed, is considered robust.

The robustness of a Trading System is measured in terms of continuity, not only with respect to the past, but also with respect to market changes.

Knowing how to manage risk is a fundamental characteristic of every good Trading System, in order to protect the available capital. Risk management depends on the ability of the signals to close an open position on the market at the most opportune moment, depending on whether it generates profits or losses.

Finally, to be valid, the Trading System must be completely mechanical and nondiscretionary. Each decision must be delegated by the trader to the automated system, which takes decisions objectively through a coded logical method, tested on a historical series of market data of interest.

Regardless of the choice on the type of Trading System, there are key points that must be set on any automated system.

First of all it is essential to set up the so-called inside bar. This is a very important pattern for any trader as it allows us to identify a slowdown typical of the market that precedes a very active phase, whether up or down, by a short period of time. The inside bar is nothing but a sensitive narrowing of the range in which you are operating. Setting this pattern is perhaps one of the most complicated points in the entire Trading System realization process and requires a certain degree of knowledge of the programming language used. If properly coded, the insid bar is essential for any type of Trading System as it identifies the best time to enter the market.

A second element to set in your automated system, following an accurate market analysis, is that of trading hours. It is in fact fundamental to define the optimal trading time slot for a specific market, so as to be able to make the most of its strategy. Furthermore, trading in a time that is not appropriate could generate unwanted losses, as the designed Trading System is not able to obtain the maximum return from the algorithms, due to the inconsistent trend trend.

Finally, it is essential to opt for a specific oscillator depending on the method with which you intend to enter and exit the market. Each oscillator has its strengths and weaknesses, which can be partially filled by the addition of other types of indicators that act as support during the course of trading operations. For example, a Dynamic

Breakout oscillator requires a volatility indicator, especially during the lateral phases of the market, which allows a narrow range to be identified both at the time of entry and of exit. Generally the latter is even more contained than the first, therefore easily identifiable in the series.

To understand if the Trading System thus built is valid, it is necessary to carry out the necessary tests.

3.2 – Logical schemes and testing

To build any type of Trading System it is necessary to define a precise logical path that takes into consideration certain fundamental points for the realization of a successful software.

Naturally the first phase consists in the market analysis. This step should not be underestimated, as each trader must be aware of the rules on which the entire financial system is based, but also the competitors with whom he will have to confront and every other stakeholder present within the reference sector. It is essential to inform yourself about what has characterized the market in its historical series, the ideas that influenced it and those that have achieved greater success rates. To undertake a trading activity with a detailed knowledge of the reference market means to start off considerably.

But analyzing the market also means defining what the objectives to be achieved are. Setting a goal also means setting aside the illusions and relying on concrete and realistic data, which are supplied directly by the market. In addition, the trader is required to decide which is the overall portfolio he intends to have in order to carry out the trading activity in the medium-long term and what is the maximum loss limit he is willing to tolerate, in order to avoid it running the risk of a real financial crisis. Every choice must be made in a rational way, to avoid squandering the entire allocated capital, lacking a correspondence between strategy and reality.

Once the market has been analyzed in detail, it is possible to move on to a second phase, namely the interpretation of the same. Based on the data collected, the trader is asked to understand, in a completely intuitive way, what the trend of the trend may be. To verify that the strategy can work in the market it is necessary to assume a range in the graph relating to the trend of the trend, verifying its efficiency. Naturally it is possible to carry out a verification of this kind only in the short term, but it is however a first step towards the awareness of the quality of the algorithm devised. If the results obtained are relatively good, it is possible to continue towards the next logical scheme, otherwise it is mandatory to re-examine the initial idea.

The next step instead involves the construction of some signals of exit from the market, which allow to manage both the profit and the losses. This phase is considered by many trading experts as the most important of the entire process of building a Trading System and therefore requires concentration and application. Exit signs must be carried out following a single purpose, namely profit maximization. It is important to analyze the behavior of the output signals both separately and in the generality of the strategy. In both cases, each signal must demonstrate consistency with the strategic idea and with the intended objectives. These tests are only indicative and are made not to understand the real effectiveness of the algorithm, but to help the trader to verify that the road taken is the correct one.

Only after defining and testing the output signals is it possible to refine the quality of the input signals by applying filters, which have the purpose of decreasing the operations, ie the inputs, excluding all operations that could lead to negative results. In this case, however, there is the risk of also excluding the signals that would have led to profits, so the application of the filters must be a well-studied operation. For best results it is always advisable to carry out tests to verify that the insertion of the filters does not alter the previous behavior of the signals. Also in this case the test must be carried out both on the individual filters and on the totality of the same. To avoid this operation taking too long, the tests must be short and fast. The insertion of the signals and the relative filters inevitably entails the realization of a series of corrections, necessary to make the entire algorithm more efficient.

Once the inclusion of logical schemes is complete, it is possible to move on to the actual testing phase. This process aims to optimize the trading strategy, thanks also to the use of databases. These allow to identify the merits and defects of the algorithm, but also the sectors in which the best results should be achieved through the built Trading System, the markets that generate losses and negative transactions and even the ideal percentage of risk depending on the quantity of operation imposed on the automated system.

The optimization phase of the Trading System mainly concerns the execution of various attempts concerning the modification of the algorithm inputs, with consequent testing of the results for each test. Input variation can be done individually or by correcting multiple values simultaneously.

It is important to choose a type of testing, among the many present in this sector, that provides objective data on the quality of the realized Trading System. In particular, testing is aimed at verifying the presence of so-called overfittings: these elements indicate the possibility that the Trading System is suitable for a past trend, but prove to be not very suitable to anticipate the correct trend of the trend in the future. Solving these problems can increase the level of robustness of the strategy and prevent any drawdown in the future.

One of the most efficient tests is called "in sample / out of sample". This test consists of the division into two different parts of a database related to a historical series of a given financial instrument. The first part, which corresponds to 70% of the database, constitutes the foundation of the entire Trading System and in it all the signals, the filters and the Money Management of the algorithm are defined. The remaining part of the database is instead used to simulate sudden future events in order to test the reactivity of the algorithm.

Testing is also essential to define the maximum limit to be set for losses. The limit always used in the Trading System corresponds to a value equal to twice the maximum drawdown level recorded in the entire historical series. This reasoning, although correct, has led to very large losses among traders over the course of the story, sometimes leading to a deep financial crisis. On the other hand, however, setting a lower level seems completely pointless.

Once the testing phase is completed, the creation of the Trading System can be considered complete. However, the real testing process is represented by the real market. In fact, each trading system requires an adaptation phase, during which the trader will have to monitor the operation of the algorithm and its efficiency. One of the features that requires the most attention is respect by the Trading System in the medium term of the established strategy.

3.3 – Possible mistakes to avoid

Many traders believe that the most serious errors occur during the trading system programming phase. In reality the greatest difficulties are detected following the principle of system construction, that is when the trader is called to identify the initial idea on which to base the entire strategy. Furthermore, traders tend not to fully satisfy all the requirements that an excellent strategy must possess, and generally from this it follows that the algorithm can prove to be not very robust, not long lasting and not suitable to adapt to all the fluctuations of the trend. The problem represented by the difficulty of the computer language, on the other hand, can be overcome with the simple aid of expert programmers, already familiar with the world of trading, able to bring the idea expressed by the trader back into the Trading System.

A trap in which traders must not fall concerns the possibility of being deceived by possible errors committed in the coding phase, which can make results be clearly better than those initially hypothesized. In reality it is a clear imprecision, verifiable also through specific tests, which concerns events that could not have any manifestation in a real market.

A further obstacle is the bouncing tick. This is an error that can positively alter the tests, but which has negative consequences once used in the trading activity. This bug involves the modification of the historical data of the series, with the consequent alteration of the point of trailing stop. The problem arises because the Trading System does not recognize the movement of the series and runs the trend in the opposite direction to the standard one. Also in this case the recognition of the error resides in the possibility of guessing that the results obtained in the various tests are excessively positive, compared to those obtainable in the real market.

Significantly insisting on the testing phase is the only way to understand, before investing real and non-virtual money, if the algorithm has some flaws. The history of trading, however, teaches that sometimes some alleged errors in the planning or construction phase of the Trading System have proved to be valid successful techniques, which over the years have spread among all traders, improving the relationship between return and risk and consequently, the entire investment activity. The wrong codes, therefore, can turn out to be real fortunes, which will still have to be tested in the real world to be able to define them as such. Precisely for this reason the job of the trader practically never ends. Once a Trading System has been created, the goal is to understand its weaknesses and strengths, to be able to build one that can always be better. It is in fact wrong to always work on the same automated system, as it is possible that bugs are created that instead of improving the trading activity lead to deteriorations, sometimes even sensitive, with the risk of seeing the work hitherto carried out in vain.

Conclusions

As seen in the previous chapters, the Trading System is the instrument that acts as a compass in the insidious world of finance and trading. In fact, trading without a valid automatic support tool, but relying only on improvisation and luck, can be harmful. Relying on a Trading System and acquiring a valid Money Management is the starting point for achieving the goals set and success in the financial market.

Although trading is a real job, it is true that almost all those who carry out online financial transactions also carry out other types of work simultaneously. At this point the problem of how to reconcile work with trading is born. To do this, it is recommended to set up a trading plan based on free time from work, considering however that the Trading System platforms are active 24 hours a day, 7 days a week, depending on the parameters set. Thanks to these systems, the trader can in fact save a lot of time, as it is not necessary for him to remain in front of the computer for hours, and it is also possible to set pre-orders for the performance of operations, which the system will manage in a completely autonomous manner . If, on the other hand, you do not want to make use of existing systems, but prefer to build the Trading System, the time to devote to the activity must necessarily be greater, especially in the implementation phase and in the previous study.

Trading online, as discussed above, has both positive and negative aspects. In fact, not everything you read on the web reflects reality, and can easily confuse those who have no experience in the sector. To protect against scams and deceptions, it is important not to rely on the first system you come across, but rather to analyze the characteristics and qualities of multiple systems, comparing them. However, profits will not be guaranteed in any case if the trading activity is not accompanied by a constant commitment and long waits, since in the short term only small results can be obtained that will be exhausted in a very short time: it is indeed in the long term that the most significant and satisfying results are shown, following hard market analysis work.

The best strategy to "win" is therefore to plan one's own strategy.

www.ingramcontent.com/pod-product-compliance
Lightning Source LLC
Chambersburg PA
CBHW070420220526
45466CB00004B/1474